T0368597

METUSELA ALBERT

WHOSE WRITINGS ARE CALLED – "THE SPIRIT OF PROPHECY" AS MENTIONED IN REVELATION 19:10???

(NOT THE WRITINGS OF MRS. ELLEN G. WHITE)

To order additional copies of this book, contact:
Xlibris
844-714-8691
www.Xlibris.com
Orders@Xlibris.com

ISBN: Softcover   979-8-3694-3296-9
         EBook   979-8-3694-3297-6

Print information available on the last page

Rev. date: 11/01/2024

Contents

Revelation 19:10 – (KJV).

v.10. And I fell at his feet to worship him. But he said unto me, "See that thou do it not! I am thy fellow servant and one of thy brethren, who hold to the testimony of Jesus. <u>Worship God! For the testimony of Jesus is the spirit of prophecy."</u>

....
....
....

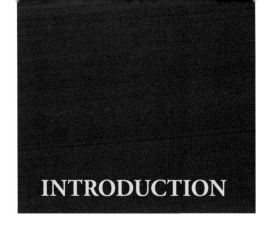

INTRODUCTION

This subject is so vital for us to clarify. WHY? Because the Seventh-Day Adventist (SDA) Church claims that <u>the writings of Mrs. Ellen G. White are the Spirit of Prophecy, mentioned in Revelation 19:10</u>.

WHAT ELSE?

The SDA Church also claims that <u>Mrs. Ellen G. White was a Prophetess of GOD</u>.

....
....
....

Therefore, this Book is written to clarify that <u>the writings of the Prophets of the Old Testament, are the Spirit of Prophecy, mentioned in Revelation 19:10</u>. In other words, the writings of Mrs. Ellen G. White, are <u>NOT</u> the Spirit of Prophecy, mentioned in Revelation 19:10.

Once we prove the false interpretation of Revelation 19:10 by the SDA Church, in order to justify Mrs. Ellen G. White as a Prophetess, that should tell you that the SDA Church surely must have had other false doctrines.

In fact, the SDA Church has 20+ False Teachings. This will stun you, and the nominal SDA members who failed to read the Scriptures in the Context.

I will deal with the 20+ False Teachings of the SDA Church in another Book. So, stay tuned and check this website for other Books that I have written, for your information – www.xlibris.com. You can also find my other Books on other online Book Sellers.

This Book is intended to tell the truth and to expose the expose the errors; to reveal how Churches failed to interpret Scripture correctly.

....

....

....

THE TRUTH versus THE ERROR.

THE TRUTH IS:

- **The writings of the Old Testament Prophets, are the Spirit of Prophecy, mentioned in Revelation 19:10.**

THE ERROR IS:

The writings of Mrs. Ellen G. White, are the Spirit of Prophecy, mentioned in Revelation 19:10.

Compiled by: Metusela F. Albert.

....

....

....

CHAPTER 1

THE TORAH

To a Jew, the <u>first Five Books</u> of the Bible is called – <u>THE TORAH</u>.

WHAT ARE THE <u>FIRST FIVE</u> BOOKS?

1. **Genesis**
2. **Exodus**
3. **Leviticus**
4. **Numbers**
5. **Deuteronomy**

....
....
....

The Jews believed that GOD (ELOHIM/ YAHWEH / JEHOVAH) that was written in <u>the TORAH</u>, was <u>the only GOD</u>. When the Jews talk of GOD, they refer to the GOD of Abraham, Isaac, and Jacob. They also refer to the GOD of the children of Israel who wrote the Ten Commandments on two tablets of stone, at Mt. Sinai.

They believed that there was <u>only One GOD</u> that existed from eternity. Actually, they <u>never heard</u> of <u>a TRINITY GOD</u> or <u>a TRIUNE GOD</u>.

NOTE: THE JEWISH PEOPLE AND MOST PROFESSED CHRISTIANS IN THE 21ST. CENTURY, STILL DO <u>NOT KNOW</u> THAT JESUS, WHOM THE PHARISEES AND SADDUCEES PLOTTED AND KILLED BY THE ROMAN SOLDIERS AT CALVARY, WAS THE GOD OF ABRAHAM WHO CAME IN HUMAN FLESH THROUGH MARY AT BETEHLEHEM.

THE TRUTH IS:

JESUS WAS <u>NOT</u> A TRINITY GOD. THERE WAS <u>NO SUCH THING</u> AS A TRINITY GOD, IS SITTING ON THE THRONE, IN HEAVEN. AND THERE WAS <u>NO SUCH THING</u> AS A TRINITY GOD HAD A BEGOTTEN SON, IN HEAVEN. AND THERE WAS <u>NO SUCH THING</u> AS A TRINITY GOD SENT A BEGOTTEN SON FROM HEAVEN, TO DIE AT CALVARY.

I know this Book will rock the minds of many mainline Denominational / Church Leaders and Pastors who failed to understand JESUS, who was the everlasting Father who became the Son of GOD, <u>by Incarnation</u> through Mary at Bethlehem – (Isaiah 43:10-11; 9:6; 7:14).

....
....
....

CHAPTER 2

THE GOD OF ADAM AND EVE WAS <u>NOT</u> A TRINITY GOD.

Please take time to read Genesis Chapters 1 and 2.

....
....
....

Read the CONTEXT in a CHRONOLOGICAL ORDER.
TAKE NOTE OF THE PRONOUN "HE"

- Read : Genesis 1:1-5 . . . He.
- Read – Genesis 1:10 . . . He.
- Read – Genesis 1:16 . . . He.
- ....
- Read – Genesis 1:26, . . . WHO WAS ELOHIM TALKNG TO?

- Read – Genesis 1: 27, 29, 31. . . He.
- Read – Genesis 2:1-3. . . . He.

NOTE: The same GOD who created heaven and earth including Adam and Eve, in six days and rested on the seventh day, was THE LORD of the Sabbath day. <u>HE WAS JESUS.</u>

JESUS was **<u>not</u>** a TRINITY GOD.

THE LORD of the Sabbath day <u>INCARNATED</u> into human flesh through Mary at Bethlehem, and <u>became the Son of GOD</u>. IF JESUS did not incarnate into human flesh, then He would <u>not</u> be able to die at Calvary, as our Savior / Sin Bearer.

I pray and hope that Christianity will come to terms and understand the purpose of the INCARNATION process, was to enable ELOHIM, the CREATOR, to die at Calvary, as our SAVIOR.

Please go and read Isaiah 44:6, 24 and 49:16.

JESUS, WHO SPOKE TO PROPHET ISAIAH, CREATED HEAVEN AND EARTH <u>BY HIMSELF</u>. DID YOU GET THAT? I HOPE SO.

NO TRINITY GOD CREATED HEAVEN AND EARTH. NO SON OF GOD EXISTED IN HEAVEN FROM ETERNITY.

IMPORTANT POINT: GOD DID <u>NOT</u> SEND A SON FROM HEAVEN, TO DIE AT CALVARY, AS OUR SAVIOR.

GET THIS:

GOD CAME DOWN BY THE <u>INCARNATION PROCESS THROUGH MARY</u> AT BETHLEHEM, AND <u>BECAME THE SON OF GOD</u>. WE ARE TALKING OF ONE PERSON IN HERE; NOT TWO PERSONS.

GOD THE FATHER BECAME THE SON OF GOD.

,,
,,
,,

CHAPTER 3

THE GOD OF NOAH WAS <u>NOT</u> A TRINITY GOD…

Please read Genesis Chapter 6 and learn <u>the Singular Pronouns</u> that refer to GOD, who spoke to Noah to build an Ark, to prepare for the flood.

Let's read Genesis Chapter 6:1-22

1. And it came to pass, when men began to multiply on the face of the earth and daughters were born unto them,

² that the sons of God saw the daughters of men, that they were fair; and they took for themselves wives of all whom they chose.

³ And **<u>the Lord said</u>**, "<u>**My** Spirit</u> shall not always strive with man, for he also is flesh; yet his days shall be a hundred and twenty years."

⁴ There were giants on the earth in those days; and also after that, when the sons of God came in unto the daughters of men and they bore children to them, the same became mighty men who were of old, men of renown.

⁵ And God saw that the wickedness of man was great in the earth, and that every imagining of the thoughts of his heart was only evil continually.

⁶ And <u>the Lord</u> repented that <u>He</u> had made man on the earth, and it grieved <u>Him</u> in <u>His</u> heart.

⁷ And <u>the Lord said</u>, "<u>I</u> will destroy man whom <u>I</u> have created from the face of the earth, both man and beast, and the creeping thing and the fowls of the air, for I repent that I have made them."

⁸ But Noah found grace in the eyes of the Lord.

⁹ These are the generations of Noah. Noah was a just man and perfect in his generations, and Noah walked with God.

¹⁰ And Noah begot three sons: Shem, Ham, and Japheth.

¹¹ The earth also was corrupt before God, and the earth was filled with violence.

¹² And God looked upon the earth, and behold, it was corrupt; for all flesh had corrupted his way upon the earth.

¹³ And God said unto Noah, "The end of all flesh has come before Me, for the earth is filled with violence through them; and behold, I will destroy them with the earth.

¹⁴ Make thee an ark of gopherwood; rooms shalt thou make in the ark, and shalt cover it within and without with pitch.

¹⁵ And this is the fashion which thou shalt make it of: the length of the ark shall be three hundred cubits, the breadth of it fifty cubits, and the height of it thirty cubits.

¹⁶ A window shalt thou make for the ark, and to a cubit shalt thou finish it above; and the door of the ark shalt thou set in the side thereof; with lower, second, and third stories shalt thou make it.

¹⁷ And behold, I, even I, do bring a flood of waters upon the earth to destroy all flesh wherein is the breath of life from under heaven; and every thing that is on the earth shall die.

¹⁸ But with thee will I establish My covenant; and thou shalt come into the ark, thou and thy sons, and thy wife and thy sons' wives with thee.

¹⁹ And of every living thing of all flesh, two of every sort shalt thou bring into the ark to keep them alive with thee; they shall be male and female.

²⁰ Of fowls after their kind, and of cattle after their kind, of every creeping thing of the earth after his kind, two of every sort shall come unto thee to keep them alive.

²¹ And take thou unto thee of all food that is eaten, and thou shalt gather it to thee; and it shall be food for thee and for them."

²² Thus did Noah; according to all that God commanded him, so did he.

....
....
....

Dear Reader,

Try and read the Singular Pronouns in GENESIS CHAPTER 6.

THE GOD OF NOAH WAS NOT A TRINITY GOD.

- Let's read Genesis Chapter 6:1-22
- 1. And it came to pass, when men began to multiply on the face of the earth and daughters were born unto them,
- 2 that the sons of <u>God saw</u> the daughters of men, that they were fair; and they took for themselves wives of all whom they chose.
- 3 And <u>the Lord said</u>, "<u>My Spirit</u> shall not always strive with man, for he also is flesh; yet his days shall be a hundred and twenty years."
- 5 And <u>God saw</u> that the wickedness of man was great in the earth, and that every imagining of the thoughts of his heart was only evil continually.
- 6 And <u>the Lord</u> repented that <u>He</u> had made man on the earth, and it grieved <u>Him</u> in <u>His</u> heart.
- 7 And <u>the Lord said</u>, "<u>I</u> will destroy man whom <u>I</u> have created from the face of the earth, both man and beast, and the creeping thing and the fowls of the air, for <u>I</u> repent that <u>I</u> have made them."

NOTE: THE GOD OF NOAH WAS THE CREATOR. HE ALONE CREATED HEAVEN AND EARTH. SINCE JESUS WAS THE CREATOR, THEREFORE, THE GOD OF NOAH WAS <u>NOT</u> A TRINITY GOD.

CHECK OUT THE <u>SINGULAR PRONOUNS</u> IN VERSES 3, 6, AND 7.

....
....
....

JESUS WAS THE GOD OF NOAH. . . . JESUS WAS <u>NOT</u> THE SON OF NOAH'S GOD. THIS POINT MUST BE CLEAR.

FURTHERMORE, THERE WAS <u>NO</u> SUCH THING AS A TRINITY GOD. AND THERE WAS <u>NO</u> SUCH THING AS THE HOLY SPIRIT IS A THIRD PERSON, IN HEAVEN.

....

....

....

CHAPTER 4

THE GOD OF ABRAHAM WAS <mark>NOT</mark> A TRINITY GOD.

Read Genesis 12:1-3. Take note of the <u>Singular Pronouns</u> used. The I pronoun, was used 4 Times.

1. Now <u>the Lord</u> had said unto Abram, "Get thee out of thy country, and from thy kindred and from thy father's house, unto a land that **<u>I</u> will show thee.**

² And **<u>I</u> will make of thee a great nation, and <u>I</u> will bless thee and make thy name great; and thou shalt be a blessing.**

³ And **<u>I</u> will bless them that bless thee, and curse him that curseth thee; and in thee shall all families of the earth be blessed."**

NOTE: THE GINGULAR PRONOUN "I" WAS USED 4 TIMES.

THE GOD OF ABRAHAM WAS **NOT** A TRINITY GOD.
READ GENESIS 12:1-3.
TAKE NOTE OF THE "I" PRONOUN USED 4 TIMES.

- 1. Now the LORD had said unto Abram, "Get thee out of thy country, and from thy kindred and from thy father's house, unto a land that I will show thee.

- 2 And I will make of thee a great nation, and I will bless thee and make thy name great; and thou shalt be a blessing.

- 3 And I will bless them that bless thee, and curse him that curseth thee; and in thee shall all families of the earth be blessed."

Compiled by: Metusela F. Albert.

Check it out for yourself and stop being fooled by your Church.

....
....
....

CHAPTER 5

THE GOD OF MOSES WAS <u>NOT</u> A TRINITY GOD.

JESUS was the "<u>I AM THAT I AM</u>", who spoke to Moses at the burning bush. – Exodus 3:13-14; John 5:39, 46; 8:58.

Exodus 3:13-14 - King James Version

¹³ And Moses said unto God, "Behold, when I come unto the children of Israel and shall say unto them, 'The God of your fathers hath sent me unto you,' and they shall say to me, 'What is His name?' what shall I say unto them?"

¹⁴ And God said unto Moses, "I Am That I Am." And He said, "Thus shalt thou say unto the children of Israel, 'I Am hath sent me unto you.'"

....
....
....

In JOHN 5:39 – JESUS said, "Search the Scriptures; for in them ye think he have eternal life; but they are they which testify of me."

In JOHN 5:46 – JESUS said, "Had ye believed Moses, ye would have believed me; for Moses wrote about me."

In John 8:58, JESUS said, "Before Abraham was, I am."

12

．．．

．．．

．．．

DID YOU NOTICE? JESUS WAS THE GOD OF ABRAHAM <u>PRIOR</u> TO HIS INCARNATION INTO HUMAN FLESH THROUGH MARY AT BETHLEHEM.

．．．

．．．

．．．

CHAPTER 6

THE GOD OF ISAIAH WAS <u>NOT</u> A TRINITY GOD.

Read Isaiah 43:10-11, 15, 16. King James Version

[10] "Ye are My witnesses," saith the Lord, "and My servant whom I have chosen, that ye may know and believe Me, and understand that I am He. Before Me there was no God formed, neither shall there be after Me.

[11] I, even I, am the Lord, and besides Me there is no savior.

,,,
,,,
,,,

[15] I am the Lord, your Holy One, <u>the Creator</u> of Israel, your King."

[16] Thus saith the Lord, who maketh a way in the sea and a path in the mighty waters,

....
....
....

Isaiah 44:6.

6 "Thus saith the Lord, the King of Israel, and his Redeemer, the Lord of hosts: <u>I am the First, and I am the Last, and besides Me there is no God.</u>

Isaiah 44:24

24 "Thus saith the Lord, thy Redeemer, and He that formed thee from the womb: <u>I am the Lord that maketh all things, that stretcheth forth the heavens alone, that spreadeth abroad the earth by Myself;</u>

....
....
....

NOTE: The GOD of Prophet Isaiah created heaven and earth by himself. That means, No Trinity GOD created heaven and earth.

The GOD of Prophet Isaiah was the Savior. JESUS alone was the Savior. Scripture is so clear, yet too many Churches continue to believe in a TRINITY GOD theory.

THE GOD OF PROPHET ISAIAH.
Read Isaiah 44:6, 24; 49:16.
HE WAS JESUS.

- 6 "Thus saith the LORD, the King of Israel, and his Redeemer, the LORD of hosts: I am the First, and I am the Last, and besides Me there is no God.

- ....

- 24 "Thus saith the LORD, thy Redeemer, and He that formed thee from the womb: I am the LORD that maketh all things, that stretcheth forth the heavens alone, that spreadeth abroad the earth by Myself;

- ....

- Isaiah 49:16.
- 16 Behold, I have graven thee upon the palms of My hands; thy walls are continually before Me.

Compiled by: Metusela F. Albert.

....
....
....

THE GOD OF PROPHET ISAIAH DECLARED THAT HE ALONE CREATED HEAVEN AND EARTH.

THAT MEANS, THERE WAS NO SUCH THING AS A TRINITY GOD. AND THERE WAS NO SUCH THING AS THE HOLY SPIRIT WAS A THIRD PERSON.

....
....
....

CHAPTER 7

A BRIEF TIMELINE OF BIBLICAL EVENTS <u>FROM</u> CREATION.

....
....
....

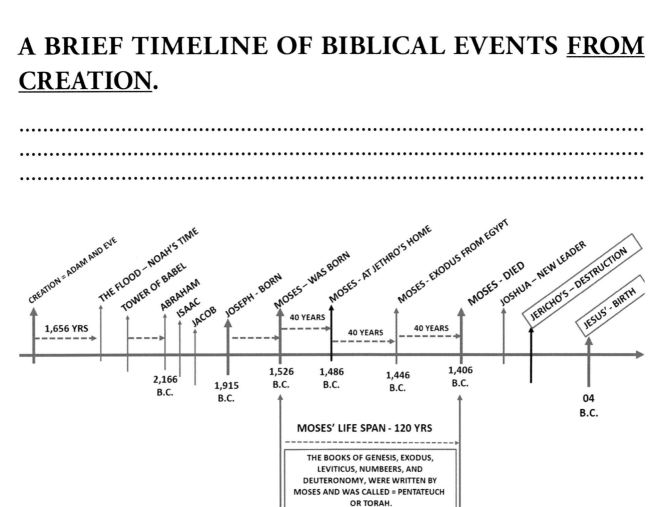

CREATION = ADAM AND EVE

THE FLOOD – NOAH'S TIME

TOWER OF BABEL

ABRAHAM

ISAAC

JACOB

JOSEPH - BORN

MOSES – WAS BORN

MOSES - AT JETHRO'S HOME

MOSES - EXODUS FROM EGYPT

MOSES - DIED

JOSHUA – NEW LEADER

JERICHO'S – DESTRUCTION

JESUS' - BIRTH

1,656 YRS

40 YEARS

40 YEARS

40 YEARS

2,166 B.C.

1,915 B.C.

1,526 B.C.

1,486 B.C.

1,446 B.C.

1,406 B.C.

04 B.C.

MOSES' LIFE SPAN - 120 YRS

THE BOOKS OF GENESIS, EXODUS, LEVITICUS, NUMBEERS, AND DEUTERONOMY, WERE WRITTEN BY MOSES AND WAS CALLED = PENTATEUCH OR TORAH.

Compiled by: Metusela F. Albert

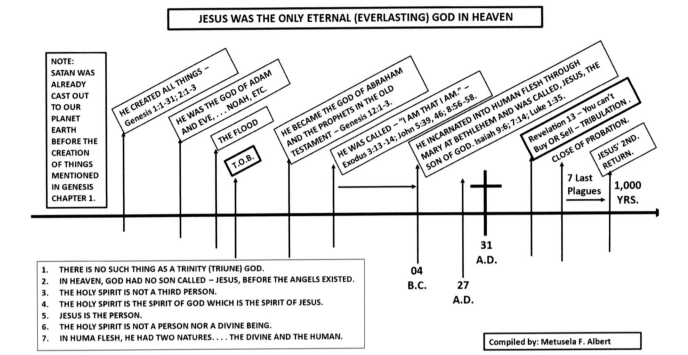

JESUS WAS THE ONLY ETERNAL (EVERLASTING) GOD IN HEAVEN

NOTE: SATAN WAS ALREADY CAST OUT TO OUR PLANET EARTH BEFORE THE CREATION OF THINGS MENTIONED IN GENESIS CHAPTER 1.

HE CREATED ALL THINGS – Genesis 1:1-31; 2:1-3

HE WAS THE GOD OF ADAM AND EVE, . . . NOAH, ETC.

THE FLOOD

T.O.B.

HE BECAME THE GOD OF ABRAHAM AND THE PROPHETS IN THE OLD TESTAMENT – Genesis 12:1-3.

HE WAS CALLED – "I AM THAT I AM." – Exodus 3:13 -14; John 5:39, 46; 8:56-58.

HE INCARNATED INTO HUMAN FLESH THROUGH MARY AT BETHLEHEM AND WAS CALLED, JESUS, THE SON OF GOD. Isaiah 9:6; 7:14; Luke 1:35.

Revelation 13 – You can't Buy OR Sell – TRIBULATION.

CLOSE OF PROBATION.

JESUS' 2ND. RETURN.

7 Last Plagues

1,000 YRS.

04 B.C.

27 A.D.

31 A.D.

1. THERE IS NO SUCH THING AS A TRINITY (TRIUNE) GOD.
2. IN HEAVEN, GOD HAD NO SON CALLED – JESUS, BEFORE THE ANGELS EXISTED.
3. THE HOLY SPIRIT IS NOT A THIRD PERSON.
4. THE HOLY SPIRIT IS THE SPIRIT OF GOD WHICH IS THE SPIRIT OF JESUS.
5. JESUS IS THE PERSON.
6. THE HOLY SPIRIT IS NOT A PERSON NOR A DIVINE BEING.
7. IN HUMA FLESH, HE HAD TWO NATURES. . . . THE DIVINE AND THE HUMAN.

Compiled by: Metusela F. Albert

THE WAS NO SUCH THING AS A TRINITY GOD.

....

....

....

CHAPTER 8

GOD DID <u>NOT</u> HAVE A BEGOTTEN SON, IN HEAVEN.

....

....

....

JESUS WAS THE GOD OF ABRAHAM WHO TOOK HUMAN FLESH THROUGH MARY AT BETHLEHEM.

THE GOD OF ABRAHAM DID <u>NOT</u> HAVE A SON IN HEAVEN CALLED - JESUS.

NOTE: JESUS WAS THE GOD OF ABRAHAM WHO HUMBLY TOOK HUMAN FLESH THROUGH MARY AT BETHLEHEM.

THIS WAS THE INCARNATION PROCESS.

Read - Genesis 1:1-31; 2:1-3; Exodus 3:13-14; 6:1-3; Isaiah 43:10-11; 44:6, 24; 49:16; John 5:39, 46; 8:56-58; Revelation 21:6-7.

....

....

....

CHAPTER 9

THE HOLY SPIRIT IS <u>NOT</u> A THIRD PERSON, IN HEAVEN.

WHO WAS THE HOLY SPIRIT?

The HOLY SPIRIT was the Spirit of GOD, which was the Spirit of JESUS. – Read Genesis 1:2.

The HOLY SPIRIT was not a person. JESUS was the person.

NOTE: IT IS THE BELIEF IN THE TRINITY GOD, THAT LEADS MOST PEOPLE TO BELIEVE IN THE HOLY SPIRIT, AS A THIRD PERSON, IN HEAVEN.

CHAPTER 10

THE TRINITY GOD THEORY IS <u>ANTI-CHRIST</u>.

When you believe in a TRINITYGOD theory, you are against JESUS CHRIST. You have demoted JESUS to a creature with a beginning, instead of He being the everlasting GOD, who had no beginning and no ending. It is that simple.

THE TRINITY GOD THEORY IS ANTI-CHRIST.

- The <u>Trinity</u> GOD theory promotes the idea that JESUS cannot be GOD by himself; for he must be added to <u>another Two Divine Beings; the Father and the Holy Spirit, to make one GOD.</u>
- They call it – "THREE IN ONE."
- 1 + 1 + 1 = 1 GOD.
- THE TRINITY GOD THEORY IS ANTI-CHRIST.

Compiled by: Metusela F. Albert.

....
....
....

CHAPTER 11

JOHN <mark>CONTRADICTED</mark> GENESIS 1:1 AND ISAIAH 43:10-11, 15.

John 1:1-3; 3:16.

....
....
....

CHAPTER 12

PAUL <u>CONTRADICTED</u> GENESIS 1:1 AND ISAIAH 43:10-11, 15.

Colossians 1:15-18.

Hebrews 12:2.

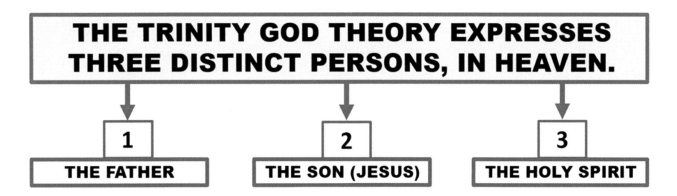

THE TRINITY GOD THEORY EXPRESSES THREE DISTINCT PERSONS, IN HEAVEN.

1	2	3
THE FATHER	THE SON (JESUS)	THE HOLY SPIRIT

ACCORDING TO PAUL, IN ROMANS 12:1-3, JESUS WAS SITTING ON THE RIGHT HAND OF THE FATHER ON THE THRONE, IN HEAVEN.

PAUL CONTRADICTED REVELATION 4:1-11; AND 21:5-7.

Compiled by: Metusela F. Albert.

....
....
....

CHAPTER 13

JESUS WAS THE ALPHA AND OMEGA, THE FIRST AND THE LAST.

Revelation 21:5-7.

The Trinity GOD theory contradicted Revelation 21:5-7.

JESUS WAS THE ALPHA AND OMEGA. HE WAS <u>NOT</u> A TRINITY GOD.

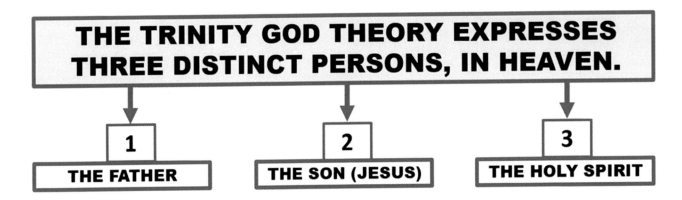

THE TRINITY GOD THEORY EXPRESSES THREE DISTINCT PERSONS, IN HEAVEN.

1	2	3
THE FATHER	THE SON (JESUS)	THE HOLY SPIRIT

ACCORDING TO PAUL, IN ROMANS 12:1-3, JESUS WAS SITTING ON THE RIGHT HAND OF THE FATHER ON THE THRONE, IN HEAVEN.

PAUL CONTRADICTED REVELATION 4:1-11; AND 21:5-7.

Compiled by: Metusela F. Albert.

24

CHAPTER 14

JESUS WAS NOT A TRINITY GOD.

CHAPTER 15

THE WRITINGS OF ELLEN G. WHITE, ARE <u>NOT</u> THE SPIRIT OF PROPHECY.

WHOSE WRITINGS ARE CALLED –
"THE SPIRIT OF PROPHECY,"
AS MENTIONED IN REVELATION 19:10???
<u>NOT</u> MRS. ELLEN G. WHITE'S.

....

NOTE: It was the writings of the Old Testament Prophets.

Compiled by: Metusela F. Albert.

....
....
....

- **·THE CHURCH OF GOD WAS FOUNDED BY JESUS CHRIST, FROM THE TIME OF CREATION.**
- **·HE IS THE HEAD OF THE CHURCH.**
- ....
- **· BUT THE SDA CHURCH WAS FOUNDED BY MRS. ELLEN G. WHITE AND HER FRIENDS (THE SDA PIONEERS), IN 1863 A.D.**
- ....
- **· Therefore, the SDA Church is NOT GOD'S Church because it teaches a TRINITY GOD, and it only started, in 1863 A.D.**
- **· Genesis 1:1-31; 2:1-3; Exodus 3:13-14; Isaiah 43:10-11; 44:6, 24; 49:16; John 5:39, 46; 8:56-58; Revelation 21:5-7.**

Compiled by: Metusela F. Albert.

Try and read Chapters 16, 17, and 18, of this Book.

....

....

....

CHAPTER 16

THE <u>INVESTIGATIVE JUDGEMENT</u> DOCTRINE BY ELLEN G. WHITE IS <u>UNBIBLICAL</u>.

The Investigative Judgment doctrine originated by Mrs. Ellen G. White. Only the SDA Church teaches this doctrine.

You can read this doctrine in Mrs. Ellen G. White's Book – The Great Controversy. Here is the Brief History about this doctrine.

After the Great Disappointment on OCTOBER 22, 1844 A.D., Mrs. Ellen G. White fabricated this doctrine. Well, what happened on OCTOBER 22, 1844 A.D.?

In America, in the early 1840s, Mr. William Miller who was a Baptist Preacher, was preaching that JESUS will return on OCTOBER 22, 1844 A.D. His hermeneutics was taken from the 2,300 Day Prophecy, in Daniel 8:13-14; which began in 457 B.C. and ended on October 22, 1844 A.D. This was the Day of Atonement, where the High Priest enters the Most Holy Place of the Sanctuary- (Exodus 25:8).

He concluded that JESUS will return on October 22, 1844 A.D. This convinced a lot of people. Among those who attended and believed was Miss Ellen Gould Harmon and her family. She was about 17 years of age, around 1844 A.D.

When JESUS did <u>not</u> return, the group disintegrated into small groups. Ellen G. Harmon was with a group called <u>Advent </u>Believers. Later she married Mr. White and became Mrs. Ellen G. White. In April 1863 A.D., she and her husband, and some others in their group, founded the Seventh-Day Adventist Church. They believed in the Seventh-day of the week as the Sabbath; and the return of JESUS, but no set time. She had dreams and visions, and became a prominent person among the group. And she wrote many Books. For example, she wrote –

> i. Patriarchs and Prophets,
> ii. Prophets and Kings,
> iii. Desire of Ages,
> iv. Acts of the Apostles,
> v. The Great Controversy.
> vi. Steps to Christ.
>
> She also wrote the Book called –
> STORY OF REDEMPTION, and many more.

In those <u>Books</u>, she was consistent in her Belief about the FATHER, THE SON, AND THE HOLY SPIRIT.

She advocated in those Books:

1. That JESUS was the Son of GOD in heaven before the angels were created.
2. That the GOD of Abraham was the only GOD in heaven.
3. That the HOLY SPIRIT was a person; a third person that existed in heaven.
4. That the FATHER, THE SON, AND THE HOLY were three Distinct Persons in heaven, yet <u>only One GOD</u>.

....

....

....

CHAPTER 17

THE <u>FALSE TEACHINGS</u> OF MRS. ELLEN G. WHITE.

Mrs. White, wrote - "Christ was the Son of God; He had been one with Him before the angels were called into existence." SOURCE: <u>Patriarchs and Prophets</u>, page 38.

According to her, JESUS AND GOD, existed from the beginning before JESUS created the angels in heaven. In other words, JESUS, existed as the Son of GOD, which means – JESUS was <u>not</u> the GOD of Abraham, but <u>the Son of Abraham's GOD</u>.

Mrs. Ellen G. White <u>did not know</u> that JESUS was the GOD of Abraham, the Creator, of heaven and earth. Because she did not understand it, thus, the SDA Church <u>did not understand</u> it, as well. That is the reason the SDA Church continues to believe in the TRINITY GOD theory.

....
....
....

Try and read what Mrs. Ellen G. White, wrote in her Book – Story of Redemption.

THE FALSE TEACHING OF MRS. WHITE ABOUT THE FATHER AND JESUS.

- Mrs. White, wrote – "After the earth was created, and the beasts upon it, <u>the Father and the Son carried out their purpose</u>, which was designed before the fall of Satan, to make man in their own image. They had wrought together in the creation of the earth and every living thing upon it. And now <u>God said to His Son</u>, "Let us make man in our image."
- SOURCE: Story of Redemption, page 20.

Compiled by: Metusela F. Albert.

According to Mrs. Ellen G. White in the statement above, the Father and the Son (JESUS) made the plan of Salvation before Lucifer's fall. The Father and His Son, created our planet earth. That contradicted Genesis 1:1.

Another error, she advocated is this: the Father and the Son were <u>Two Distinct Beings</u> before the Creation of our planet earth.

....
....
....

THE FALSE TEACHING OF MRS. WHITE ABOUT JESUS.

- # 4 – Mrs. White, wrote. " Lucifer in heaven, before his rebellion, was a high and exalted angel, next in honor to God's dear Son . .
- Christ, God's dear Son, had the preeminence over all the angelic host. He was one with the Father before the angels were created . . . The great Creator assembled the heavenly host, that He might in the presence of all the angels confer special honor upon His Son.
- The Son was seated on the throne with the Father, and the heavenly throng of holy angels was gathered around them. The Father made known that it was ordained by Himself that Christ, His Son, should be equal with Himself, so that wherever was the presence of His Son, it was as His presence. The Word of the Son was to be obeyed as readily as the word of the Father. .. . Lucifer was envious and jealous of Jesus Christ."
- SOURCE: Story of Redemption, pages 13-14.

Compiled by: Metusela F. Albert.

....
....
....

Another FALSE Teaching. According to Mrs. Ellen G. White, the Father and the Son were seated on the Throne, in heaven. This is a clear contradiction of Revelation Chapter 4:1-11, where GOD alone is sitting on the Throne, in heaven.

....
....
....

MRS. WHITE'S FALSE BELIEF ABOUT "THE SEAL OF GOD".

•She wrote. "The Sabbath is the seal of God."

- SOURCE: THE GREAT CONTROVERSY, page 608.

....

NOTE: She was promoting the idea that a person will be Sealed for Observing the SABBATH. Nonsense!

Compiled by: Metusela F. Albert.

MRS. ELLEN G. WHITE WROTE – THE SABBATH IS GOD'S SEAL, IN HER BOOK – THE GREAT CONTROVERSY, PAGE 608. THAT IS UNBIBLICAL.

ACCORDING TO HER, THE ONE WHO KEEPS THE SABBATH COMMADMENT WILL BE SEALED. BUT THERE ARE TEN COMMANDMENTS, NOT ONE COMMANDMENT. SHE CONTRADICTED BY ADVOCATING - ONE COMMANDMENT TO BE KEPT.

If Mrs. Ellen G. White was correct, then expect all Jews who called on the Roman Governor, Pilate to release Barabbas, instead of JESUS, to be sealed and taken to heaven.

THAT IS INSANE.

....
....
....

She also wrote that – the Father, the Son (JESUS), and the Holy Spirit, are three distinct persons in heaven.

- **MRS. WHITE WAS ANTI-CHRIST.**

  ....

- Mrs. White, wrote – "**. . . There are three living persons of the heavenly trio.** In the name of these three powers, - the Father, the Son, and the Holy Ghost, those who receive Christ by living faith are baptized, and these powers will cooperate with the obedient subjects of heaven in their efforts to live the new life in Christ."
- **BIBLE TRAINING SCHOOL, VOL 1V, FEBRUARY 1906, # 9.**

  ....

NOTE: MRS. WHITE believed in three persons existing in heaven, and making up one GOD. . . In other words, SHE did NOT believe that JESUS was GOD by himself, the Alpha and Omega.

Compiled by: Metusela F. Albert

....

....

....

CHAPTER 18

<u>THE WRITINGS OF THE PROPHETS OF THE OLD TESTAMENT</u>, <u>ARE THE SPIRIT OF PROPHECY</u>.

In John 5:39, JESUS SAID, "SEARCH THE SCRIPTURES; FOR IN THEM YE THINK YE HAVE ETERNAL LIFE; BUT THEY ARE THEY WHICH TESTIFY OF ME."

....
....
....

At the time when JESUS spoke those words recorded in John 5:39, the Old Testament was the Scripture. Thus, the 66 Books of the Old Testament testified of JESUS. Therefore, the <u>66 Books of the Old Testament</u> are the Spirit of Prophecy, mentioned in Revelation 19:10.

....
....
....

NOTE: We have proven that the writings of Mrs. Ellen G. White are **not** the Spirit of Prophecy, as mentioned in Revelation 19:10. Therefore, the SDA Church who advocated her writings to be <u>the Spirit of Prophecy</u>, mentioned in Revelation 19:10, <u>is incorrect, and heretical.</u>

SO, WHAT IS THE BOTTOMLINE ABOUT THE SDA CHURCH?

Surely, the SDA Church has a problem with false Interpretation of Scripture. It is a serious issue.

DID YOU NOTICE??? . . . The SDA Church promoted Mrs. Ellen G. White to be their Prophetess, but the MORMON CHURCH (LDS) promoted Mr. Joseph Smith, as their Prophet. Both Denominations are wrong. Wrong! Wrong! Wrong!

Dear folks, Telling the Truth is <u>not</u> Hate Speech. Telling the truth is to help others to stop being deceived by their Churches / Denominations.

....

....

....

WHOSE WRITINGS ARE CALLED –

"THE SPIRIT OF PROPHECY," AS MENTIONED IN REVELATION 19:10???

NOT MRS. ELLEN G. WHITE'S.

....

NOTE: It was the writings of the Old Testament Prophets.

Compiled by: Metusela F. Albert.

....
....
....

BEFORE I CLOSE THIS CHAPTER. HERE IS ANOTHER QUESTION THAT NEEDS TO BE CLARIFIED.

IN REVELATION CHAPTER 10; WHO WAS ASKED TO GO AND TAKE THE LITTLE BOOK FROM THE ANGEL THAT HAS ONE LEG ON THE LAND, AND ONE LEG ON THE SEA? WAS IT THE DISCIPLE JOHN? OR MRS. ELLEN G. WHITE, WHO WAS ASKED TO TAKE THE BOOK AND EAT IT?

ANSWER: JOHN WAS THE ONE TO TAKE THE LITTLE BOOK FROM THE ANGEL, AND EAT IT. JOHN WAS THE LAST OF THE DISCIPLES TO DIE. HE WAS IMPRISONED ON THE ISLAND OF PATMOS BECAUSE OF HIS FAITH IN JESUS CHRIST. HE WROTE THE BOOK OF REVELATION ABOUT 95 A.D. OR 96 A.D.

JOHN WAS TO PROPHESY AGAIN. AND JOHN WAS THE ONE WHO WROTE THE BOOK OF REVELATION. THE BOOK OF DANIEL PROPHESIED ALREADY ABOUT THE LITTLE HORN POWER; AND REVELATION WAS WRITTEN TO PROPHESY <u>THE SECOND TIME</u> ABOUT THE LITTLE HORN POWER WITH THE NUMBER OF ITS NAME = 666 (Revelation 13:15-18).

....
....
....

I UNDERSTAND THAT THE SDA CHURCH CLAIMS THAT MRS. WHITE WHO EXPERIENCED THE GREAT DISAPPOINTMENT ON OCTOBER 22, 1844 A.D., WAS THE ONE TO TAKE THE BOOK AND EAT IT; AND PROPHECY AGAIN. THE MESSAGE OF JESUS CHRIST'S RETURN ON OCTOBER 22, 1844 A.D., WAS SWEET TO HER, BUT BECAME BITTER IN THE STOMACH, AFTER JESUS DID <u>NOT</u> RETURN. THE SDA CHURCH'S INTERPRETATION SOUNDS VERY CONVINCING, BUT OUT OF CONTEXT.

HERE IS THE TRUTH WHERE MOST SDA MEMBERS FAILED TO REASON. THE BOOK OF REVELATION WAS THE LAST BOOK OF THE NEW TESTAMENT. THE BIBLE CLOSES WITH 66 BOOKS. AND MRS. ELLEN G. WHITE'S WRITINGS WERE NOT PART OF THE BIBLE. HER WRITINGS WERE **NOT** THE SPIRIT OF PROPHECY, MENTIONED IN REVELATION 19:10.

....
....
....

CONCLUSION.

THIS BOOK YOU ARE READING IS <u>MY 18TH BOOK</u> I HAVE WRITTEN ON RELIGIOUS ISSUES THAT ARE CONTROVERSIAL WITH A LOT OF MISINFORMATION.

Thank you for taking the time to read this Book. I hope this Book is of help to increase your faith in the writings of the Prophets of the OLD TESTAMENT, which testified about JESUS.

When you fully understand who JESUS was in the Old Testament, you will <u>not</u> believe in <u>Mrs. White's writings</u> as the Spirit of Prophecy, mentioned in Revelation 19:10, as promoted by the SDA Church. And you will <u>not</u> believe in <u>Mr. Joseph Smith's writings, as promoted by the Mormon Church (LDS CHURCH)</u>.

Don't forget to memorize Genesis 1:1 and Isaiah 43:10-11, 15. These Scriptures will expose the misinformation spewed out by the mainline Denominations, Pastors, Bishops, Evangelists, Elders, and Church Leaders.

REMEMBER: JESUS was the CREATOR of heaven and earth. HE was the only GOD, who is sitting on the Throne, in heaven. HE took human flesh by incarnation through Mary, at Bethlehem, and became the Son of GOD, to save us from eternal damnation.

REMEMBER: JESUS WAS NOT A TRINITY GOD. JESUS DOES NOT HAVE TO BE ADDED TO THE FATHER AND THE HOLY SPIRIT TO MAKE ONE GOD. JESUS WAS GOD BY HIMSELF. HE WAS SELF-EXISTENT.

THERE IS NO SUCH THING AS – THE FATHER + JESUS (THE SON) + THE HOLY SPIRIT = 1 GOD.

Read my other Books online – www – Xlibris.com. Check also the other online Book Sellers.

PUBLISHED ON MARCH 04, 2011

PUBLISHED ON JUNE 01, 2021

....
....
....

WHAT IS THE TRUTH?

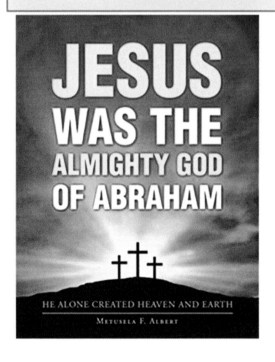

• Most Professed Christians and Protestant Churches have not understood yet that JESUS who became our Sin Bearer at Calvary (31 A.D.) was the Almighty God of Abraham who created heaven and earth.

THERE IS NO TRINITY GOD IN HEAVEN.

BOOK - PUBLISHED ON DECEMBER 16, 2020

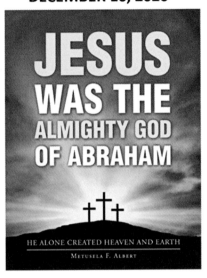

BOOK - PUBLISHED ON JANUARY 22, 2021

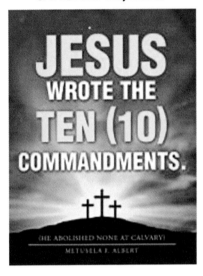

BOOK - PUBLISHED ON SEPTEMBER 12, 2021

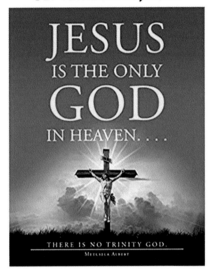

....
....
....

PUBLISHED ON AUGUST 17, 2021.

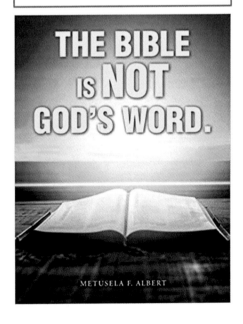

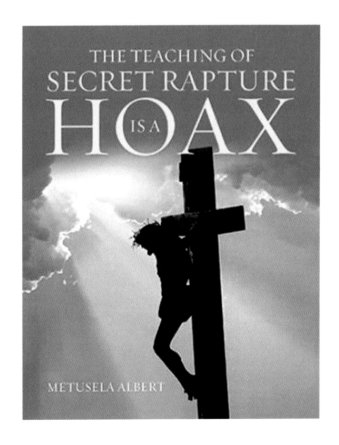

BOOK # 8

PUBLISHED ON MARCH 21, 2023.

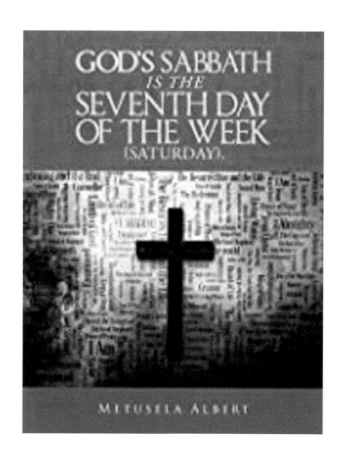

. . . .
. . . .
. . . .

MY **9TH BOOK** – WAS PUBLISHED ON NOVEMBER 21, 2023. . . .
It is available at -
www.Xlibris.com AND at other online Book Sellers.

THIS IS A BOOK THAT YOU CANNOT JUDGE BY ITS COVER. . .

YOU NEED TO READ IT.

CHRISTIANITY FAILED TO UNDERSTAND THE CONTRADICTIONS BY JOHN, PAUL, ETC.

GOD DID NOT CONTRADICT WHAT HE SAID TO THE PROPHETS.

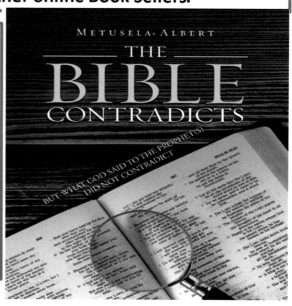

Those FIVE BOOKS will also reiterate the TRUTH that – JESUS, was and is, the Only GOD, in heaven.

JESUS WAS <u>NOT</u> A TRINITY GOD.

Therefore, by June 30, 2025, I would have completed <u>23 Published Books</u>, registered at the Library of Congress, USA.

I, AS <u>THE AUTHOR</u> OF THOSE BOOKS, MUST GIVE GOD THE GLORY.

Without JESUS CHRIST, I can do nothing. All my achievements are by the Grace of JESUS CHRIST. HE gave me the wisdom and the strength, to write those Books, to uplift Him, <u>our only GOD</u>. While writing about the Truth, at the same time, the errors must be exposed.

REMEMBER THIS, IF YOU BELIEVE IN A TRINITY GOD, <u>THUS, YOU ARE ANTI-CHRIST</u>. YOU HAVE DEMOTED JESUS, THE ONLY EVERLASTING GOD, TO A CREATURE WITH A BEGINNING AND AN ENDING.

WARNING: Anyone who believes in the writings of Mrs. Ellen G. White as the Spirit of Prophecy, mentioned in Revelation 19:10, is <u>ANTI-CHRIST</u>. Because, indirectly, you are against the writings of the Prophets in the Old Testament Books, which testified about JESUS CHRIST. It is that simple!

WHOSE WRITINGS ARE CALLED –

<u>"THE SPIRIT OF PROPHECY,"</u> AS MENTIONED IN REVELATION 19:10???

<u>NOT</u> MRS. ELLEN G. WHITE'S.

....

NOTE: It was the writings of the Old Testament Prophets.

Compiled by: Metusela F. Albert.

THE END.

Printed in the United States
by Baker & Taylor Publisher Services